Country CRAFTS

Country CRAFTS

Creative ideas for
decorations, displays and gifts
on a country theme

Tessa Evelegh

ACROPOLIS
BOOKS

First published in 1996 by
Ultimate Editions
an imprint of
Anness Publishing Limited
Boundary Row Studios
1 Boundary Row
London SE1 8HP

This edition exclusively distributed in Canada by Book Express, a division
of Raincoast Books Distribution

ISBN 1-86035-034-8

Publisher: Joanna Lorenz
Project editor: Lindsay Porter
Designer: Janet James
Photographer and stylist: Michelle Garret
Illustrator: Nadine Wickenden

Topiary tree on p 9 created by Terence Moore
Photographs on pp 90−1 by James Duncan
Styling on pp 90−1 by Tessa Evelegh

Printed in Singapore by Star Standard Industries Pte. Ltd.

Previously published as part of *Glorious Country*

Contents

Introduction

In recent years, the relaxed, weathered and natural look characterized by country style has become increasingly popular, extending through every area of the house, from wall and floor coverings, to curtains, bed linen and other accessories. This organic, informal style is also reflected in other details throughout the home — in the insistence on fresh, seasonal ingredients in cooking, in a renewed interest in age-old crafts to decorate the home, and especially in flower arranging. Gone are the formal arrangements of the past and rules of symmetry and colour no longer apply. There is even a no-holds barred approach to materials: any natural objects — such as fir cones, nuts and twigs, even brightly coloured vegetables straight from the garden — can be used to create beautiful gifts and arrangements for every area of the home. ❧ The joy of working with natural materials has many benefits — which provides some explanation for the popularity of the country look in general. People may have become disillusioned with the bustle and speed of modern life, and whether they live in a town house, flat, or country cottage, dream of a slower, gentler era, which allowed time to savour the passing seasons and enjoy the company of friends and family. You may not be able to live in the cottage of your dreams, but the country style is open to everyone. Incorporate some of these elements into your home, to create a restful and welcoming environment. Create a topiary tree from dried seedheads and spices, and the scent will fill the air; replace your kitchen table with scrubbed pine, and hang lavender hearts on the walls, scent drawers with dried-flower sachets and light your rooms with candles in wooden candlesticks. You don't have to live in the country to create the look: it comes from a way of thinking as much as from a way of living. ❧ This book shows you how to get into that way of thinking, and how to channel it into creative projects that will bring something of the dream of

BELOW: The heart is a popular folk-art motif. This paper gift box has been embellished with a small posy of dried flowers and herbs, tied with a bow.

country living into your home – whether that is a farmhouse or a flat. But it's not just the end-product of your creativity that you will value; in the process of designing and making country-style artefacts and effects you will find a satisfaction and sense of peace that are the real goals of country style. Country style has many interpretations and all over the world there are towns-people who dream of a calmer way of life in a place where traffic doesn't bustle, the air is clean and night skies are filled with stars, not neon. This may be an idealized picture, but it has an underlying truth: country life is still governed by seasonal changes, not man-made deadlines.

ABOVE: *Fresh flowers and herbs make a delightful combination in a summer basket or tied in a posy.*

  Country homes are alive, growing and comfortable and country crafts are for living with, not just looking at. Many of the effects that we think of as talismans of country style have an eminently practical function.   Country style may vary a lot, according to nationality and the local climate, but there is a core of recognizable elements. It is a home-made, functional, comfortable style. There is often a big kitchen area, with a large scrubbed pine table and an assortment of comfortable chairs. Country kitchens can be a riot of pattern and colour, where the dresser is stacked with displays of china and the beams are hung with baskets full of drying flowers and herbs. Bunches of fresh herbs should never be hidden away in cupboards, so use them to make a pretty and practical display out of 'head banging' reach. Work surfaces need to be practical, tough and easy to keep clean, but their severity can be

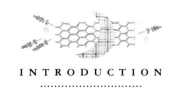

softened with fresh or dried natural materials. ❧ The flowers that decorate the country kitchen are simple and unpretentious, and vary with the seasons – dried flowers, ivy, nuts and berries in the winter and meadow-fresh wild flowers in the summer. You can use attractive, ornamental cabbages, for a truly individual country look, and use raffia and wheat for a rustic wreath. ❧ Throughout the home, flower arrangements take their cue from nature and are combined with other organic materials to provide a more casual, spontaneous look than hot-house blooms. A ginger jar that has been in the family for years might stand alongside an enamel jug filled with flowers from yesterday's walk. You might choose to float flowerheads on a glass plate, or collect supple twigs to form a heart-shaped wreath wrapped with trailing ivy. The colours of autumn may be represented by gourds, vegetables and dried seedheads. ❧ The country home is not a fashion statement, and its colour schemes should reflect the natural colour in the landscape; these need not be dull, bland and safe; they can be as rich as autumn, with touches of brilliance, or warm as a summer pasture filled with buttercups or a field of ripe corn. ❧ The house responds to personal touches; a sleep pillow made from chamomile and hops will add a relaxing ambiance to a bedroom. Make time in your life to be creative, even if it just means placing a handful of flowers into a jar. All home-made embellishments add richness to the home and give you a sense of personal achievement that money cannot buy. ❧ This book includes step-by-step projects to suit all levels of experience and creative ability. You may feel daunted by needlework but more confident about making pictures with leaves and hand-made paper; unsure about flower arranging, but

BELOW: *Little circles of unbleached muslin enclose an aromatic mixture of chamomile, rosemary and lavender. Hang under hot running water in the bath to release the scent.*

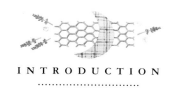

ABOVE: *Table-top topiary brings an almost everlasting natural element indoors. Here, a florist's dry foam ball was attached to the top of a length of tree trunk, fitted into a terracotta pot and covered with bunches of dried oregano. Moss at the base of the trunk covers the fixings.*

able to pop a few dried flowerheads into a terracotta pot. Whatever you choose, rest assured that all the projects have been designed to give maximum effect for minimum effort. If you want to brighten up your kitchen very quickly, bind up some fresh herbs and flowers in a traditional tussie mussie, or show off sticks of cinnamon and red chillies in a decorative spice pot. You can share the joy of country style by making gifts — from a bathtime treat jar to aromatic rosemary-flavoured olive oil.   When it comes to choosing materials for your craft projects take a tip from the squirrel and start hoarding! There are so many second-hand stores, car boot sales and jumble sales around, and if you buy things that have potential, you will always have something to hand when the creative mood strikes. It can be amazingly difficult to find a wooden basket or a nice fabric remnant when you want one, so have a 'potential' corner in the loft or the shed, and keep it well stocked!   On a very practical note, the materials you will need are easy to find and use. Florist's foam, chicken-wire, raffia and tissue paper are all available from florists and craft shops.   Whether you go for the total country look for your home, or just a few details, always try to decorate in a way that is sympathetic to the character and age of your house. Use the best features, so decorate an interestingly shaped window, for example, to create a focal point; be courageous about showing off the fruits of your labour. Your home should please you, and country style is about personal touches, natural materials, warmth and comfort. So, follow your instincts and enjoy the charm of country life.

Fresh from the Fields

Nothing captures the mood of the season better than bringing a little of the outdoors inside. Glean flowers, herbs and greenery from your own garden, the hedgerows, the fields, and even the market-place; gather together a few simple containers to put your treasures in; and then enjoy the abundance of seasonal colours, textures and aromas.

Fresh Herb Wreath

Gather together a basketful of sweet fresh herbs and make them into an aromatic wreath, to hang in the kitchen or to use as a decorative garland for a celebration. If you choose the fleshier herbs — which hold their moisture — and spray the wreath well, it should last for a couple of days; after this you may wish to dismantle it and dry the individual bunches of herbs.

MATERIALS

*florist's wire
scissors
fresh sage
fresh or dried lavender
fresh parsley
hot glue gun and glue sticks
wreath base, about 30 cm / 12 in
diameter
fresh chives
raffia*

1

Using the florist's wire, wire all the herbs except the chives into generous bunches.

2

Using the glue gun, fix two bunches of sage to the wreath base, stems pointing inwards.

3

Next, fix enough lavender bunches side by side to cover the width of the wreath base, hiding the sage stems. Attach bunches of parsley to cover the lavender stems in the same way.

4

Work around the wreath base in this way until it is generously covered by the herbs.

5

Wire the chives into four generous bunches and trim the cut ends straight. Form each pair into a cross and bind it with raffia. Wire the crosses into position.

6

Tie raffia around the wreath at intervals. Make a raffia hanging-loop, thread this on to a generous bundle of raffia at the centre top, and tie the ends of the bundle into a bow to finish.

Provençal Herb Hanging

Fix bunches of fresh herbs to a thick plaited rope, add tiny terracotta pots to give the design structure and then fill it in with garlic and colourful chillies to make a spicy, herbal gift full of Provençal flavour, for anyone who loves to cook.

MATERIALS

*hank of seagrass string
scissors
garden string
florist's wire
fresh sage
fresh thyme
fresh oregano
2 small flowerpots
6 florist's stub wires
2 garlic heads
hot glue gun and glue sticks (optional)
large dried red chillies*

1

Cut six lengths of seagrass string about three times as long as the desired finished length of the hanging. Take two lengths, fold them in half and place them under a length of garden string. Pass the cut ends over the string and through the loop of the fold, thereby knotting the seagrass on to the garden string. Repeat twice with the remaining four seagrass lengths. Divide the seagrass into three bundles of four lengths and plait them to form the base of the herb hanging.

2

Finish the end of the plait by binding it with a separate piece of seagrass string.

3

Using florist's wire, bind the herbs into small bundles and tie each one with garden string. Use this to tie them to the plaited base.

4

Wire the flowerpots by passing two stub wires through the central hole and twisting the ends together.

5

Wire the pots to the base by passing a stub wire through the wires on the pots, passing it through the plait, and then twisting the ends together.

6

Tie garden string around the garlic heads and tie these to the base. Wire or glue the chillies into position, and fill the pots with more chillies.

Fresh-flower Fruit Bowl

Make the prettiest summer fruit bowl by arranging trailing flowers and foliage through a wire basket, topping it with chicken-wire and a pretty plate, and then piling on the fresh fruit. This is a delightful touch for outdoor entertaining.

<u>MATERIALS</u>

jam jar
wire basket
fuchsia flowers or
similar trailing blooms
secateurs
chicken-wire to fit the diameter
of the basket
attractive plate to fit the
diameter of the basket
selection of colourful fruit

1

Fill the jam jar with water and place it in the centre of the basket.

2

Trim the flower stems with secateurs and arrange them all round the basket by threading the stems through the wire and into the jar of water. Continue until the flowers and foliage provide a delicate curtain of colour around the basket.

3

Cut the chicken-wire to fit over the basket and fix it by bending it around the rim. Place a plate on this chicken-wire, and then fill the plate with colourful summer fruits.

Vegetable Centrepiece

The flower stall is not the only source of material for centrepieces — the vegetable stall provides great pickings, too. Here, a still-life of ornamental cabbages — complemented by a simple cut-open red cabbage and some artichokes — makes a flamboyant focal-point for the table. The theme is carried through by adding an ornamental cabbage leaf to the cutlery bundle at each setting.

MATERIALS

dyed raffia
painted wooden basket
2 ornamental cabbages in pots
lichen moss
1 set of cutlery and napkin
per person
baby-food jar
painted trug
red cabbage, halved
globe artichokes

1

Tie a bow of dyed raffia around the handle of the wooden basket. Remove several perfect cabbage leaves and place the cabbages in their pots in the basket.

2

Cover the tops of the pots with silvery-grey lichen moss.

3

Tie up each cutlery bundle with a napkin and an ornamental cabbage leaf. Finish the arrangement by putting a few more leaves into a baby-food jar and tying dyed raffia around it. Fill a garden trug with the red cabbage halves and the globe artichokes.

Candle Centrepiece

Even the humblest materials can be put together to make an elegant centrepiece.
The garden shed has been raided for this one, which is made from a terracotta
flowerpot and chicken-wire. Fill it up with red berries, ivies and white roses
for a rich, Christmassy look; or substitute seasonal flowers and foliage
at any other time of the year.

MATERIALS

18 cm / 7 in flowerpot
about 1 m / 39 in chicken-wire
knife
florist's foam ball to fit
the diameter of the pot

beeswax candle
tree ivy
white roses
berries
variegated trailing ivy

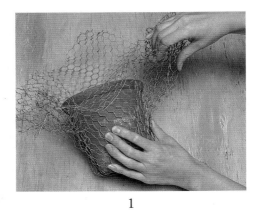

——— 1 ———

Place the pot in the centre of a large square
of chicken-wire. Bring the chicken-wire up
around the pot and bend it into position.

——— 2 ———

Cut the florist's foam ball in half and soak
one half. The other half isn't needed.

——— 3 ———

Place the foam in the pot, cut-side up
so you have a flat surface. Position the candle
in the centre of the pot.

——— 4 ———

Arrange glossy tree-ivy leaves all around the
candle, to provide a lush green base.

——— 5 ———

Add a white rose as a focal point, and
bunches of red berries among the ivy.

——— 6 ———

Add more white roses, and intersperse
trailing variegated ivy among the tree ivy.

Wild at Heart

Often, the simplest arrangements are the most appealing. Here, flowers are arranged very simply in little glass jars wound around with blue twine and carefully grouped to make a delightful still-life.

MATERIALS

blue twine	*scabious*
2 jam jars	*anemones*
secateurs	*glass plate*

1

Wrap the blue twine around the jars and tie securely. Fill the jars with water.

2

Fill one jar with scabious and another with anemones, cutting the stems to the right lengths as you go.

3

Fill the plate with water.

4

Cut one of the flower stems very short and allow the bloom to float in the plate. This is a delightful solution for any heads of flowers that have broken off during transit.

Advent Candle Ring

*An Advent candle ring makes a pretty Christmas centrepiece. This
one – decorated with glossy green tree ivy, Cape gooseberries, dried citrus-fruit
slices and bundles of cinnamon sticks – is a delight to the eye, while
giving off a rich seasonal aroma.*

MATERIALS

*florist's foam
knife
florist's ring basket
4 church candles
moss
dried orange slices
florist's stub wires
secateurs
cinnamon sticks
golden twine
tree ivy
Cape gooseberries*

1

Soak the florist's foam and cut it to fit
the ring basket.

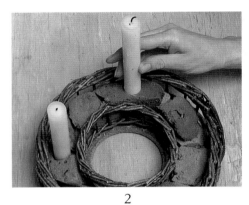

2

Position the candles in the foam.

3

Cover the florist's foam with moss, pushing
it well down at the sides of the basket.

4

Wire the orange slices by passing a stub wire
through the centre, and then twisting the
ends together at the outside edge. Wire the
cinnamon sticks into bundles, then tie them
with golden twine and then pass a wire
through the string.

5

Wire the tree-ivy leaves into bundles.

6

Position the ivy leaves into the ring. Decorate
by fixing in the orange slices and cinnamon
sticks and placing the Cape gooseberries on
top of the candle ring at intervals.

Autumn Fruitfulness

The sheer beauty of autumn produce makes it difficult to resist. It's too good to be left in the larder. Gather together all the softly bloomed purple fruits and pile them into a rich seasonal display for a side table or centrepiece.

MATERIALS

metal urn
filling material, such as
bubble-wrap, newspaper or
florist's foam
several varieties of plums
black grapes
hydrangea heads
globe artichokes
blueberries

1

Unless you have a huge abundance of fruit, fill the bottom of the urn with bubble-wrap, newspaper or florist's foam.

2

Arrange as many different varieties of plums as you can find on the filling, saving a few for the final decoration.

3

Add a large bunch of black grapes, draping them over the rim of the urn. Finish the arrangement with hydrangea heads, artichokes, scattered plums and blueberries.

Autumn Gold

The golds of autumn can be gathered into a fabulous display, using even the humblest of containers. Here, the dahlias have simply been put into a store-cupboard Kilner jar and given a seasonal necklace of hazelnuts.

MATERIALS

hazelnuts
seagrass string
secateurs
dahlias
Kilner jar
pumpkins
branches of pyracantha
with berries

	1	

Tie the hazelnuts on to the seagrass string to make a 'necklace'.

Cut about 1 cm / ½ in off the end of each dahlia stem and place the stems in the Kilner jar filled with water.

Tie the hazelnut 'necklace' around the jar. Finish the arrangement with pumpkins and pyracantha branches.

Springtime Garland

Garlands of fresh flowers make delightful decorations for any celebration.
This pretty little hanging of pansies and violas has a woodland feel that can be
re-created at any time, because these flowers are available in
most months of the year.

MATERIALS

secateurs
chicken-wire the desired length of
the garland and three times the
desired width
scissors
black plastic bin liner
about two pansy plants for every
15 cm / 6 in of garland
about six viola plants for every
15 cm / 6 in of garland
florist's stub wires
moss

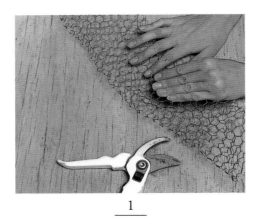

1

Using secateurs, cut the chicken-wire to size
and then form it into a flattened roll.

2

Cut the bin liner into squares large enough
to cover the rootballs of the pansies
and violas.

3

One by one, unpot each plant, gently remove
any loose soil and place the rootball in
the centre of a square of bin liner.

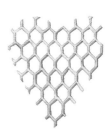

26

4

Gather the plastic around the rootball and
fix it in place by winding stub wires loosely
round the top, leaving a short length free
to fix to the garland.

5

Fix the bagged-up plants to the garland
using the free end of wire.

6

Finish off by covering any visible plastic with
moss, fixing it with short lengths of florist's
stub wire bent hairpin-style.

Summer Gift Basket

Fresh flowers are always a welcome gift — make them into something extra special by laying them in a basket with prettily packaged, home-made strawberry jam.

MATERIALS

jar of strawberry jam
pink paper
glue
paper strawberry print
scissors
glazed pink paper
raffia
wooden basket
coloured paper
roses

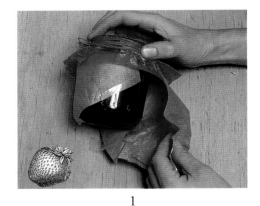

1

Make up a pretty presentation for the strawberry jam by wrapping the jar with pink paper and gluing on a paper strawberry print to fix the paper.

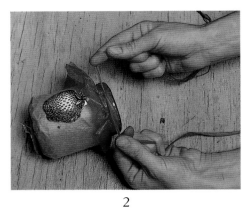

2

Make a top of glazed pink paper and a raffia tie. Line the basket with coloured paper and fill it with a bunch of roses, tied with raffia, and the strawberry jam.

Christmas Gift Basket

Decorate a willow basket with gilded ivy leaves, and then pack it with seasonal goodies: a pot of variegated ivies and berries, decorative florist's pineapples, plus a few extra treats like beeswax candles and crystallized fruits.

MATERIALS

tree ivy
picture framer's wax gilt
willow basket
scissors
hessian
pot of variegated ivy with berries
presents

1

Gild the tree ivy by rubbing on picture framer's wax gilt, using your fingers. Decorate the rim of the basket with these gilded leaves.

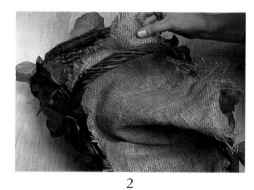

2

Cut a piece of hessian to size and fray the edges. Use it to line the basket. Add the pot of ivy, plus presents to fill the basket.

Twiggy Door Wreath

Welcome seasonal guests with a door wreath that's charming in its simplicity. Just bend twigs into a heart shape and adorn the heart with variegated ivy, berries and a Christmas rose, or substitute any pure-white rose.

MATERIALS

*secateurs
pliable branches, such as
buddleia, cut from the garden
florist's wire
seagrass string
variegated trailing ivy
red berries
tree ivy
picture framer's wax gilt
(optional)
white rose
golden twine*

1

Using secateurs, cut six lengths of pliable branches about 70 cm / 28 in long. Wire three together at one end. Repeat with the other three. Cross the two bundles over at the wired end.

2

Wire the bunches together in the crossed-over position.

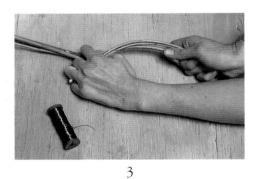

3

Holding the crossed, wired ends with one hand, ease the long end round and down very gently, so the branches don't snap. Repeat with the other side, to form a heart shape. Wire the bottom end of the heart.

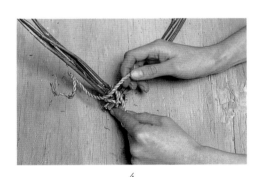

4

Bind the wiring with seagrass string at top and bottom and make a hanging loop at the top.

5

Entwine trailing ivy around the heart shape.

6

Add berries. Make a posy of tree-ivy leaves (if you like, gild them using picture framer's wax gilt) and a white rose. Tie the posy with golden twine. Wire the posy in position at the top of the heart.

Tied Posy

Flowers are at their most appealing when kept simple. Just gather together some garden cuttings and arrange them in a pretty posy that the recipient can simply unwrap and put straight into a vase, without further ado.

MATERIALS

secateurs	*scabious*
roses	*brown paper*
eucalyptus	*ribbon*

1

Using secateurs, cut each flower stem to approximately 15 cm / 6 in long.

2

Gather the flowers together, surrounding each rose with some feathery eucalyptus, and then adding the scabious.

3

Wrap the posy with paper and tie it with a pretty ribbon bow.

Tussie Mussie

Traditionally, tussie mussies were bouquets of concentrically arranged aromatic herbs that were carried around as a personal perfume. This one combines the blue-greens of sage and thyme with the soft blues of lavender and scabious flowers.

MATERIALS

6 scabious
fresh thyme
fresh lavender
fresh sage
dyed raffia

1

Encircle the scabious blooms
with fresh thyme.

2

Arrange a circle of lavender around this,
making sure the piece keeps its circular shape.

3

Add a circle of sage, then tie with a
generous bundle of dyed raffia.

Easter Display

*Coloured eggs immediately transform springtime flowers into an Easter display.
Simplicity is the secret: just gather together an abundance of flowers and add a
few eggs, carefully laid on to moss to evoke the idea of a nest.*

MATERIALS

*hard-boiled eggs
food dye if you want to eat the
eggs, or fabric dye if they are
purely for decoration
one jam jar for each colour
vinegar
salt
secateurs
tulips or any spring flowers
vase
moss
plate*

1

First wash the eggs, and then make up the
dye. Do this by emptying half a small bottle
of food dye or half a disc of fabric dye into a
jam jar, and then pouring on 300 ml /
½ pint / 1¼ cups of hot water.

2

Add 30 ml / 2 tbsp vinegar and 15 ml / 1 tbsp
salt. Lower an egg into the jam jar of dye
and leave it for a few minutes.
Check the colour regularly.

3

When the egg has reached the desired colour,
lift it out and repeat with the rest. You will
find that the more eggs you dye, the weaker
the solution will become, so you'll have to
leave the eggs in longer to achieve the
same effect. Cut about 1 cm / ½ in off the end
of each flower stem with secateurs, and
then place them in a vase. Complete the
arrangement by arranging the eggs on the
moss on a plate.

Everlasting
Treats

....

*Nature offers many exquisite textures and colours
that have natural everlasting qualities — or
that can be encouraged to have them — so scour the
countryside, dried-flower stockists, and even
your own store-cupboard for flowers, leaves, grasses
and dried whole spices; collect richly textured
strings, raffias and twines; and then transform
them into delightfully lasting natural gifts.*

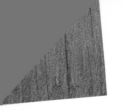
Lavender Basket

A basket decorated with bunches of dried lavender makes an exquisitely pretty aromatic linen store. It could also be kept on the kitchen dresser, filled with freshly laundered tea towels ready on hand when you need them.

MATERIALS

dried lavender (2 bunches for the handle plus about 1 bunch for every 10 cm / 4 in of basket rim)

florist's wire
scissors
willow basket

hot glue gun and glue sticks
blue paper-ribbon
blue twine

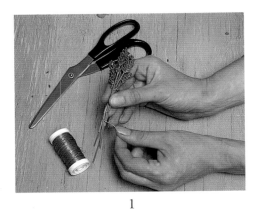

1

Wire up enough small bundles of about six lavender heads to cover the rim of the basket generously. Arrange the heads so they are staggered to give fuller cover. Trim the stalks short.

2

Wire up the remaining lavender into 12 larger bunches of about 12 lavender heads for the handles, leaving the stalks long.

3

Form a 'star' of three of the larger bunches and wire them together. Repeat with the other nine so you have four largish star-shaped bunches of lavender.

4

Fix the small bunches to the rim of the basket, using either wire or hot glue in a glue gun. Start at one end and work towards the handle. Use the bunches generously so they overlap each other to cover the width of the rim.

5

Once the rim is fully covered, glue on individual heads of lavender to cover any spaces, ugly wires or stalks. Pay particular attention to the area near the handles, because you will have finished up with quite a few bare stalks there.

6

Wind blue paper-ribbon around the handle. Wire the longer lavender bunches to the handles, leaving the stalks long but trimming to neaten them. Cut the stalks on the inside of the handle shorter to fit the space. Bind the wired joints with blue twine.

Heart of Wheat

Fashion a heart at harvest time, when wheat is plentiful, for a delightful decoration that would look good adorning a wall or a dresser at any time of the year. Despite its delicate feathery looks, this heart is quite robust and should last many years.

MATERIALS

scissors
heavy-gauge garden wire
or similar
florist's tape
florist's wire
large bundle of wheat ears

1

Cut three long lengths of heavy-gauge wire and bend them into a heart shape. Twist the ends together at the bottom.

2

Use florist's tape to bind the wire heart shape.

3

Using florist's wire, make up enough small bundles of wheat ears to cover the wire heart shape densely. Leave a short length of wire at each end for fixing to the heart shape.

4

Starting at the bottom, tape the first bundle of wheat ears to the heart.

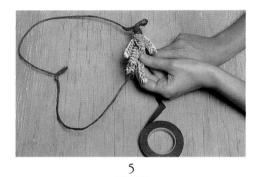

5

Place the second bundle further up the heart shape behind the first, and tape it in position. Continue until the whole heart is covered.

6

For the bottom, wire together about six bunches of wheat ears, twist the wires together and wire them to the heart, finishing off with florist's tape to neaten. This is what the back should look like by the time you've finished.

Flower Topiary

Dried flowers look fabulous when given the sculptural form of faux topiary.
These strawflowers and larkspur set into a tall cone make a stunning everlasting
display. Wrap the pot in a co-ordinating fabric to finish off the arrangement.

MATERIALS

small flowerpot
square of fabric to cover the pot
knife
small florist's dry foam cone
4 florist's stub wires
florist's dry foam cone,
about 18 cm / 7 in tall
scissors
bunch of dried blue larkspur
florist's wire, if necessary
bunch of dried
yellow strawflowers

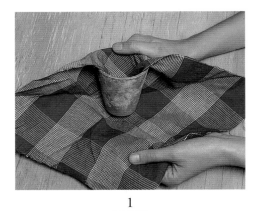

1

Stand the pot in the centre of the fabric and
tuck the corners into the pot. Tuck in any
other loose portions of fabric.

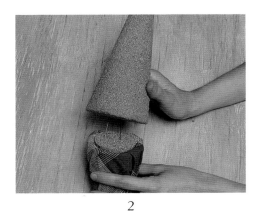

2

Cut down the small foam cone to fit the
inside of the pot. Position four stub wires
so they project above the foam. Use these
for attaching the top cone.

3

Snip the florets off the larkspur, leaving the
small stalks to push into the foam. Make four
rows of larkspur down the length of the cone
to quarter it; then fill in either side of these
rows to create broad blue bands. Many of the
florets' stalks will be strong enough to pierce
the foam. If not, wire the florets with
florist's wire. Finally, fill in the panels
with the strawflowers.

Leaf and Petal Decorations

Decorations are so much more appealing when made from all things natural.
These, made from preserved oak and beech leaves and dried hydrangea flowers,
are easy to do, and they make delightful tree or table decorations.

MATERIALS

scissors
dried mop-head hydrangeas
(about two for every ball)
hot glue gun and glue sticks
florist's dry foam balls, about
7.5 cm / 3 in in diameter
glycerined beech leaves
glycerined or dyed, dried
oak leaves
picture framer's wax gilt

1

Snip the florets off the mop-head hydrangeas.
Put aside the florets that have the prettiest
colouring on the top-side of the petals. Leave
a little stalk on these, but trim the stalks off
the rest. Carefully glue a floret top-side
down on to a florist's ball.

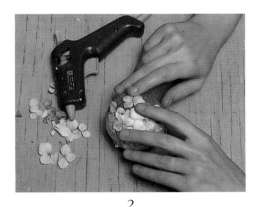

2

Continue to glue the florets face downwards
until the ball is completely covered.

3

Put a tiny spot of glue on the back of each of
the petals of a reserved floret. Fix this,
top-side up, on to the ball – over the base
covering of petals. If you leave a little stalk
on the florets you set aside for the top layer,
this can be used to help attach it to the ball.
Let the glue work just where the petals touch
the ball, allowing them to curl naturally at
the edges to provide texture. Continue until
the ball is covered. To make the leaf balls,
first gild the beech leaves with wax gilt.
Stick the beech and oak leaves over the ball,
overlapping them slightly to cover the foam.

Hydrangea Pot

Dried materials can be used to make the simplest, yet most exquisite, gifts.
Here's an easy but effective idea, using a single hydrangea head.

MATERIALS

glue
dyed, dried oak leaf
small flowerpot
dyed raffia
scissors
dried mop-head hydrangea

1

Use a spot of glue to attach the leaf to the pot,
and then tie it on with raffia. Secure the raffia
tie at the back with another spot of glue.

2

Cut the hydrangea stalk short enough so that
the head rests on the pot. Place the head
in the pot.

Spice Pots

For a cook, make a cornucopia of culinary flavourings by putting different dried
herbs and spices into terracotta pots and packing the pots in a wire basket.

MATERIALS

cinnamon sticks
dried bay leaves
garlic
dried red chillies
small flowerpots
wire basket
wire
raffia

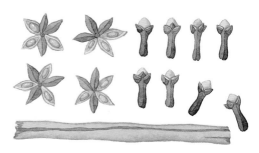

1

Place the herbs and spices in the pots and
place the pots in the basket.

2

Bend a piece of wire into a heart shape and
bind it with raffia. Leave a long end free
before starting to bind. When binding is
complete, the end can be used to tie the heart
to the basket. Finish with a bow.

Leafy Pictures

Delicate skeletonized leaves come in such breathtakingly exquisite forms that they deserve to be shown off. Mount them on hand-made papers and frame them to make simple yet stunning natural collages.

MATERIALS

wooden picture frame
sandpaper
paint
paintbrush
backing paper
pencil
scissors
skeletonized leaf
picture framer's wax gilt
hot glue gun and glue sticks
mounting paper

1

Take the frame apart and sand it down to provide a key before painting. A translucent colourwash has been used for painting here, but any paint will do.

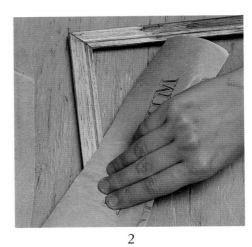

2

Allow the paint to dry, then sand the paint back so you're left with a wooden frame with shading in the mouldings, plus a veil of colour on the surface.

3

Use the hardboard back of the frame as a template for the backing paper. Draw around it with a pencil to form a cutting line.

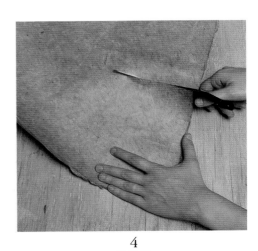

4

Cut the backing paper out.

_5_

Prepare the leaf by rubbing with picture
framer's wax gilt. This does take a little time
as the gilt has to be well worked in.

_6_

Stick the backing paper on the frame back,
glue the mounting paper in the centre and
attach the leaf on to that. Here, the leaf is
centred with the stalk breaking the edge of
the mounting paper. Finally, put the
frame back together.

Natural Christmas Decorations

Raid the store-cupboard and scrap box, add garden clippings plus dried fruit slices, and you have the ingredients for delightful Christmas decorations that can be individually hung or tied on to the tree, or strung on to twine to make a garland.

MATERIALS

*florist's stub wires
bundles of twigs
picture framer's wax gilt
dried bay leaves
dried pear slices
fabric scraps
dried apple slices
dried orange slices
small elastic bands
cinnamon sticks
gold twine
beeswax candle ends*

1

Wire together bundles of twigs, and then gild them by rubbing in picture framer's wax gilt.

2

Make up the fruit bundles. Make a small loop at one end of a florist's stub wire. Thread on some dried bay leaves, and then a dried pear, passing the wire through the rind at the top and bottom. Make a hook at the top.

3

Tie a scrap of coloured fabric to the bottom loop and a scrap of green (synthetic chiffon is shown) at the top, to look like leaves. Make the apple-slice bundles by threading on first the thick apple slices, and then the bay leaves.

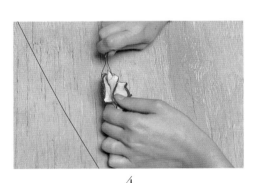

4

Wire up pairs of thinner-sliced apples by passing a wire through the centre and twisting the wires together at the top. Wire up the orange slices in the same way.

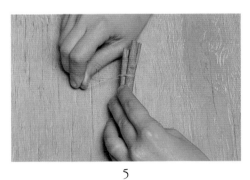

5

Use small elastic bands to make up bundles of cinnamon sticks.

6

Either hang each decoration directly on the tree or make up a garland to hang on the tree or at the window. Here, they have been strung together using gold twine. The beeswax candle-ends are simply knotted in at intervals.

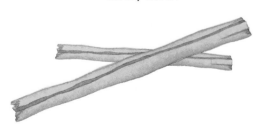

Everlasting Christmas Tree

This delightful little tree, made from dyed, preserved oak leaves and decorated with tiny gilded cones, would make an enchanting Christmas decoration. Make several and then group them to make a centrepiece, or place one at each setting.

MATERIALS

*knife
bunch of dyed, dried oak leaves
florist's wire
small fir cones
picture framer's wax gilt
flowerpot, 18 cm / 7 in tall
small florist's dry foam cone
4 florist's stub wires
florist's dry foam cone,
about 18 cm / 7 in tall*

1

Cut the leaves off the branches and trim the stalks. Wire up bunches of about four leaves, making some bunches with small leaves, some with medium-sized leaves and others with large leaves. Sort the bunches into piles.

3

Prepare the pot by cutting the smaller foam cone to fit the pot, adding stub-wire stakes and positioning the larger cone on to this. Attach the leaves to the cone, starting at the top with the bunches of small leaves, and working down through the medium and large leaves to make a realistic shape. Add the gilded cones to finish.

2

Insert wires into the bottom end of each fir cone and twist the ends together. Gild each cone by rubbing on wax gilt.

Fruity Tree

Glycerined leaves make a perfect foundation for any dried topiary. You can buy them in branches, ready glycerined for use, or glycerine your own garden prunings. Here, they have been wired into bunches for a fabulous, full look.

MATERIALS

secateurs
3 branches of glycerined beech leaves
florist's stub wires
dried pear slices
florist's dry foam ball, about 13 cm / 5 in diameter
flowerpot, 18 cm / 7 in tall

1

Cut the leaves off the branches and trim the stalks short. Wire up small bunches of four or six beech leaves and twist the ends of the wires together.

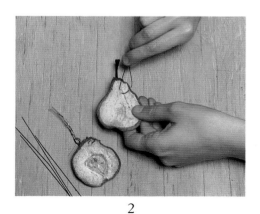

2

Pass a stub wire through the top of each pear slice and twist the ends together.

3

Completely cover the portion of the ball that will show above the pot with beech leaves.

4

Add the pear slices and put the ball into the pot.

Spice Topiary

Fashion a delightfully aromatic, culinary topiary from cloves and star anise, pot it in terracotta decorated with cinnamon sticks and top with a cinnamon-stick cross. Sticking all the cloves into the florist's foam is both easy to do and wonderfully therapeutic.

MATERIALS

*small 'long Tom'
flowerpot
knife
cinnamon sticks
hot glue gun and glue sticks
florist's dry foam cone,
about 23 cm / 9 in tall
small florist's dry foam cone
florist's stub wires
large pack of star anise
cloves*

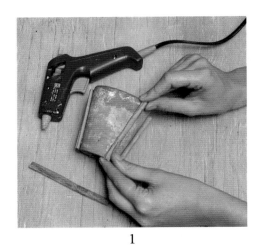

1

Prepare the pot by cutting the cinnamon sticks to the length of the pot and gluing them in position.

2

Trim the top of the larger cone. Cut the smaller cone to fit inside the pot. Put four stub-wires upright in the pot so they project above the foam.

3

Use the stub-wires to stake the trimmed cone on top of the foam-filled pot.

4

Sort out all the complete star anise from the pack, plus any that are almost complete — you'll need about 20 in all. Wire these up by passing a wire over the front in one direction, and another wire over the front in another direction to make a cross of wires. Twist the wires together at the back and trim to about 1 cm / ½ in.

EVERLASTING TREATS

5

Start by arranging the star anise in rows
down the cone – about three each side to
quarter the cone. Put two vertically between
each line. Next, just fill the whole remaining
area of cone with cloves, packing them
tightly so none of the foam shows through.

6

Glue two short pieces of cinnamon stick
into a cross. Wire this up, and use it
to decorate the top.

Dried-flower Pot

Dried flowers always look their best when the blooms are massed and the stalks not too prominent. Here's a charming treatment: roses and lavender tucked into a tiny terracotta pot, and then tied around with raffia.

MATERIALS

knife
small florist's dry foam cone
small 'long Tom' flowerpot
dried rosebuds
scissors or secateurs
dried lavender
dyed raffia
hot glue gun and glue sticks

1

Trim the foam to fit the pot. Place the rosebuds around the edge of the pot.

2

Cut the lavender stalks to about 1 cm / ½ in and use them to fill the centre of the arrangement. Tie a dyed raffia bow around the pot and secure it at the back with a spot of glue.

Everlasting Basket

*Hydrangeas look fabulous dried, providing a flamboyant display that can simply
be massed into a basket. They're also about the easiest flowers to dry at home.
Just put the cut flowers in about 1 cm / ½ in of water and leave them.
The flowers will take up the water and then gradually dry out.*

MATERIALS

*knife
florist's dry foam
painted wooden basket
dried mop-head hydrangeas
dried globe artichokes
ribbon*

_____
1

Cut the florist's foam to fit and fill the
basket, and then arrange the hydrangeas
to cover the top of the basket.

_____
2

Add the dried globe artichoke at one end
for texture.

_____
3

Tie a ribbon to the handle of the basket
to finish.

Dried-herb Wreath

A dried-herb wreath based on lavender makes a wonderful, textural, aromatic wall hanging. This one also incorporates mugwort, tarragon, lovage and large French lavender seedheads.

MATERIALS

scissors
florist's wire
dried lavender
dried mugwort
dried lovage
dried tarragon
hot glue gun and glue sticks
small wreath base
French lavender seedheads

1

Wire all the dried herbs and flowers, except the French lavender seedheads, into small bunches.

2

Using a glue gun, fix a bunch of lavender to the wreath base.

3

Next, glue a bunch of mugwort to the wreath base.

4

Work round the base, adding a bunch of lovage.

5

Continue all round the wreath, interspersing the different bunches of herbs to cover it completely, using the tarragon to add a feathery look.

6

Finally, for structure, add the individual French lavender seedheads.

Love and Kisses Collage

This witty natural collage is made from tropical seedheads and cinnamon sticks mounted on linen muslin. Even the frame has been decorated with giant cinnamon sticks, glued over a simple wooden one.

MATERIALS

*wooden picture frame
brown backing paper
scissors
linen muslin
hot glue gun and glue sticks
knife
small cinnamon sticks
florist's wire
heart-shaped or any other large
tropical seedheads
4 huge cinnamon sticks*

1

Take the glass out of the picture frame and stick the backing paper to the hardboard backing. Cut the linen muslin to size, and fray the edges. Put spots of glue all around the edge of the muslin and then stick it to the backing.

2

Glue six short lengths of cinnamon into three crosses, and then wire them up to form a delicate metallic cross joint.

3

Glue the heart-shaped seedheads to the top of the picture; glue the cinnamon 'kisses' to the bottom.

4

Finish by making a cinnamon-stick frame. Cut two huge cinnamon sticks to the same length as the frame and two to the same as the width. First glue a stick to the top of the frame, and then one to the bottom. Next, glue the side ones to these.

Decorative Dried Artichokes

The exquisite pinky shades at the base of some dried globe artichokes are too beautiful to be covered up by containers. Show them off by balancing the artichokes across pots covered in linen muslin to make wonderful natural decorations.

MATERIALS

small flowerpot
square of linen muslin
dyed raffia
dried globe artichokes with
a pinky-purple hue

1

Place the pot in the centre of the linen muslin and tuck the fabric corners into the pot.

2

Tuck in any other loose ends, and then tie everything in place with raffia. Make an arrangement by balancing the artichokes on the pot to show off the depth of colour on the undersides.

Spicy Pomander

*Pomanders were originally nature's own air fresheners. The traditional
orange pomanders are fairly tricky to do, because the critical drying process can
so easily go wrong, leading to mouldy oranges. This one, made of cloves and
cardamom pods offers none of those problems, and makes a refreshing change
in soft muted colours.*

MATERIALS

*cloves
florist's dry foam ball,
about 7.5 cm / 3 in diameter
hot glue gun and glue sticks
green cardamom pods
raffia
florist's stub wire*

1

Start by making a single line of cloves all
around the circumference of the ball.
Make another one in the other direction,
so you have divided the ball into quarters.

2

Make a line of cloves on both sides of the
original lines to make broad bands of cloves
quartering the ball.

3

Starting at the top of the first quarter,
glue cardamom pods over the foam,
methodically working in rows to create a neat
effect. Repeat on the other three quarters.

4

Tie a bow in the centre of a length of raffia.
Pass a stub wire through the knot and
twist the ends together.

5

Fix the bow to the top of the ball using the stub wire.

6

Join the two loose ends in a knot for hanging the pomander.

Country Gifts

What can bring more pleasure than gifts inspired by country traditions? They have a quality that acknowledges the seasons and withstands the test of time. Gather together all the natural materials you can find — shells, papers, natural fabrics, wire, and even chicken-wire — and turn them into something very special.

Sleep Pillow

Many people still swear by sleep pillows, which are traditionally filled with chamomile and hops. Since hops are related to the cannabis plant, they induce a feeling of sleepy well-being, while chamomile helps you to relax. Either buy ready-prepared sleep mix, or make up your own with chamomile, lemon verbena and a few hops. Stitch a pillow filled with these relaxing herbs to keep on your bed, and look forward to some good night's sleep.

MATERIALS

*linen muslin, 2 m × 20 cm /
80 × 8 in (this can be made up
of two or more shorter lengths)
pins, needle and thread
scissors
pure cotton fabric, 50 × 25 cm /
20 × 10 in
herbal sleep mix
1 m / 39 in antique lace
1 m / 39 in ribbon,
1 cm / ½ in wide
4 pearl buttons*

1

Prepare the linen muslin border by stitching together enough lengths to make up 2 m / 80 in. With right sides facing, stitch the ends together to form a ring. Trim the seam. Fold the ring in half lengthways with wrong sides facing and run a line of gathering stitches close to the raw edges.

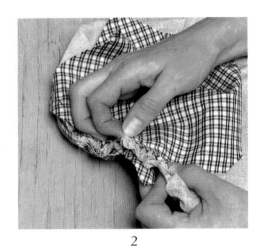

2

Cut two pieces of cotton fabric into 25 cm / 10 in squares. Pull up the gathering threads of the muslin to fit the cushion edge. Pin it to the right side of one square, with raw edges facing outwards, matching the raw edges and easing the gathers evenly round the cushion. Put the second square on top and pin the corners. Stitch the seams, leaving a gap for stuffing. Trim the seams.

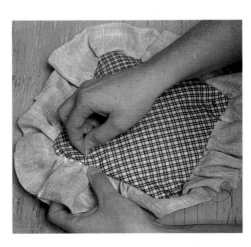

3

Turn the cushion right-side out and fill it with herbal sleep mix. Stitch the gap to enclose the border.

4

Using tiny stitches, sew the lace to the cushion about 2.5 cm / 1 in away from the border.

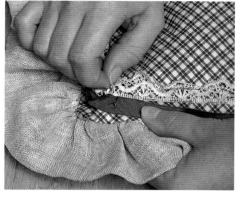

5

Stitch the ribbon close to the lace, making a neat diagonal fold at the corners.

6

Finish by sewing a tiny pearl button to each corner.

Herb Pot-mat

Protect tabletops from hot pots and pans with an aromatic mat, filled with cinnamon, cloves and bay leaves. The heat of the pot immediately releases the piquancy of its contents, kept evenly distributed with mattress-style ties.

MATERIALS

scissors
ticking, at least 62 × 55 cm /
25 × 22 in
pins, needle and thread

spice mix to fill, e.g. dried bay
leaves, cloves, cinnamon sticks
heavy-duty upholstery needle
cotton string

1

First make the hanger by cutting a strip of ticking 5 × 30 cm / 2 × 12 in. With right sides facing, fold this in half lengthways. Stitch the long side, leaving the ends open. Trim the seam. Turn right side out and press. Fold in half to form a loop. Cut two rectangles from the fabric measuring about 62 × 50 cm / 25 × 20 in.

2

Place the cushion pieces on a flat surface, right sides facing, and then slip the hanging loop between the layers, with the raw edges pointing out towards a corner.

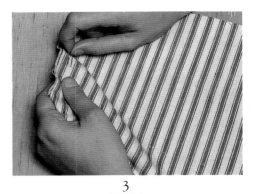

3

Pin and stitch the cushion pieces together, leaving about 7.5 cm / 3 in open. Trim the seams. Turn right side out.

4

Fill the cushion with the spices.

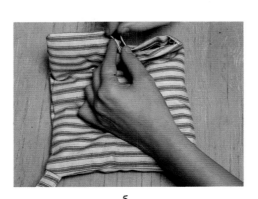

5

Slip-stitch to close the opening.

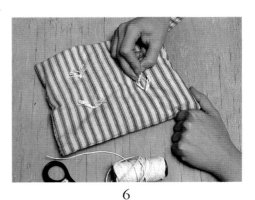

6

Using a heavy-duty upholstery needle threaded with cotton string, make a stitch about a third in from two sides of the cushion, clearing the spices inside the mat away from the area as you go. Untwist the strands of the string for a more feathery look. Repeat with three other ties to give a mattress effect. Make a simple knot in each to secure the ties.

Lavender Sachets

*Use fabric scraps to appliqué simple motifs on to charming chequered fabrics,
and then stitch them into sachets to fill with lavender and use as drawer-
fresheners. Inspired by traditional folk art, these have universal appeal.*

MATERIALS

*scissors
fabric scraps
paper for templates
pins, needle and thread
stranded embroidery thread in
different colours
loose dried lavender
button*

1

Cut two pieces of fabric into squares about
15 cm / 6 in. If you are using a checked or
striped fabric, it is a good idea to let the
design dictate the exact size. Scale up the
template and use it as a pattern to cut bird
and wing shapes from contrasting fabrics.
Pin and tack the bird shape to the
right side of one square.

2

Neatly slip-stitch the bird shape to the
sachet front, turning in the edges as you go.
Repeat with the wing shape.

3

Using three strands of embroidery thread
in a contrasting colour, make neat running
stitches around the bird and its wing.

4

Make long stitches on the tail and wing to
indicate feathers, graduating them into a
pleasing shape. Sew in the button eye.

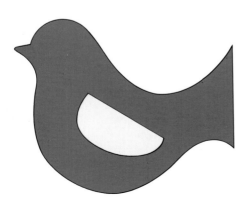

5

With right sides facing, stitch the front and
back of the sachet together, leaving a
5 cm / 2 in gap. Trim the seams. Turn it
right-side out and press. Fill with dried
lavender, and then slip-stitch to close the gap.

Lacy Lavender Heart

Evocative of the Victorian era, this exquisitely pretty heart-shaped lavender bag is made from simple, creamy muslin, and trimmed with antique lace and satin ribbon. The chiffon ribbon at the top is tied into a loop for hanging on coat hangers with favourite garments.

MATERIALS

*paper for template
scissors
silky muslin, about
60 × 20 cm / 24 × 8 in*

*pins, needle and stranded
embroidery thread
pearl button
loose dried lavender*

*50 cm / 20 in antique lace
50 cm / 20 in very narrow
satin ribbon
50 cm / 20 in medium ribbon*

1

Make a heart-shaped paper template about 15 cm / 6 in high and use this as a pattern. Cut four heart shapes from muslin. Tack the hearts together in pairs so each heart is a double thickness of muslin.

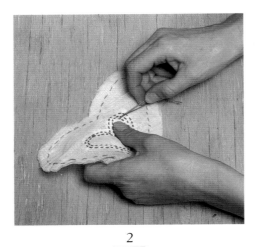

2

Cut a smaller heart shape from muslin. Carefully stitch this to the centre front of one of the larger heart shapes, using two strands of embroidery thread and a running stitch. Make another row of running stitches inside this.

3

Sew the button to the top of the smaller heart.

4

Stitch a third row of running stitches inside the other two. Allow the edges of the smaller heart to fray. With right sides facing, stitch all around the edge of the two large double-thickness muslin heart shapes, leaving a gap of 5 cm / 2 in. Trim the seams, snip into the seam at the 'V' of the heart and snip off the bottom point within the seam allowance. Turn the heart right-side out. Fill it with lavender and slip-stitch to close the gap. Don't despair if the heart looks pretty miserable and misshapen at this stage!

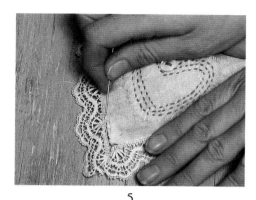

5

Carefully slip-stitch the lace around the edge
of the heart.

6

Stitch the satin ribbon over the lower edge
of the lace.

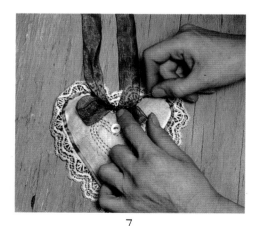

7

Finish with a ribbon bow, arranging it so the
long tails are upwards as these can then be
joined to form a loop for hanging on
coat hangers in the wardrobe.

Herb Bath-bag

Enjoy a traditional herbal bath by filling a fine muslin bag with relaxing herbs, tying it to the taps and letting the hot water run through. This draw-string design means it can be re-used time after time, if you keep refilling it with new herbs. Chamomile and hops are relaxing; basil, and sage are invigorating.

MATERIALS

silky muslin, about 30 × 40 cm / 12 × 16 in
pins, needle and thread

scissors
fabric scraps, for casing
1 m / 39 in narrow ribbon

safety pin
herb bath-mix or any combination of dried herbs

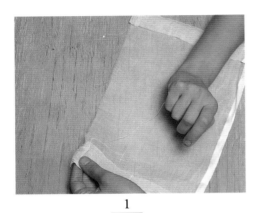

1

With right sides facing, fold over about 5 cm / 2 in of the silky muslin at both short ends, pin and stitch each side. Trim the seams. Turn right-side out.

2

Turn in and hem the raw edges of the folded-over ends.

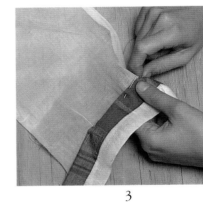

3

Cut two strips of cotton fabric about 2.5 cm / 1 in wide and as long as the width of the muslin, with about 5 mm / ¼ in extra for turnings all round. Iron a hem along both long edges. Turn in and hem the ends, then pin one casing on the right side of the muslin so the bottom edge of the casing lines up with the hem line. Neatly stitch the casing in place along both long seams. Repeat with the other casing.

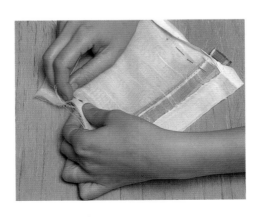

4

With right sides together, fold the muslin in half so the casings line up. Stitch the side seams from the bottom edge of the casing to the bottom edge of the bag. Trim the seams.

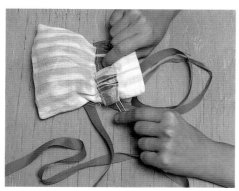

5

Cut the ribbon in half, attach a safety pin to
one end and use this to thread the ribbon
through the casing so both ends finish up at
the same side. Remove the safety pin.

6

Attach the safety pin to one end of the other
piece of ribbon and thread it through the
casing in the other direction so the ends
finish up at the other side. Fill with
herbs ready for use.

Shell Pot

Decorate a flowerpot with shells and some old netting, and then use it to hold plants, pencils, paintbrushes, strings, ribbon, or any paraphernalia that needs to be kept in check. It's a pretty and inexpensive way to make a very special container.

MATERIALS

small net bag
flowerpot, 18 cm / 7 in tall
scissors
hot glue gun and glue sticks
thick string
small cowrie shells
cockle shells
starfish or similar central motif

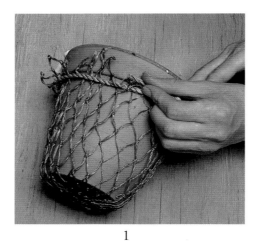

1

Slip the net bag over the flowerpot and trim the top edge. Secure it by gluing on a length of string.

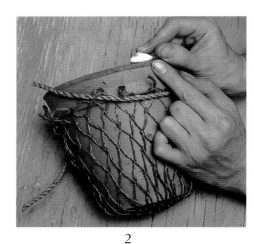

2

Using a glue gun, position a row of cowrie shells along the top edge.

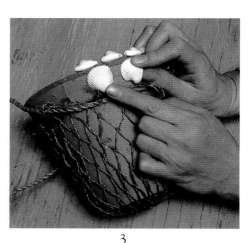

3

Glue cockle shells around the rim; position the starfish and four cockle shells at the front.

Shell Box

A simple brown-paper box takes on a South-Seas feel when decorated with half-cowries. Available from craft shops, their flattened bottoms make them easy to stick to surfaces. Here, some have also been strung together to make a toggle for fastening.

MATERIALS

hot glue gun and glue sticks
raffia
small buff box
half-cowrie shells
upholstery needle

1

Glue a loop of raffia from the bottom of the box, up the back and along the top.

2

Tie half-cowries into a bunch on a length of raffia, tying each one in separately. Leave a short length of raffia free. Pierce the front of the box with an upholstery needle and thread the raffia through. Knot it on the inside.

3

Glue on a pattern of half-cowries to decorate the outside of the box.

Shell Candle Centrepiece

An old flowerpot, scallop shells gleaned from the fishmonger or kitchen and smaller shells picked up from the beach make up a fabulous, Venus-inspired table-centrepiece. Either put a candle in the centre, as here, or fill it with dried fruits or flowers.

MATERIALS

hot glue gun and glue sticks
8 curved scallop shells
flowerpot, 18 cm / 7 in tall
bag of cockle shells
4 flat scallop shells
newspaper, florist's foam or
other packing material
saucer
candle
raffia

1

Generously apply hot glue to the inside lower edge of a large curved scallop shell. Hold it in place on the rim of the pot for a few seconds until it is firmly stuck. Continue sticking shells to the top of the pot, arranging them so they overlap slightly, until the whole of the rim has been covered.

2

In the same way, glue a cockle shell where two scallops join. Continue all around the pot.

3

Place another row of cockles at the joins of the first row. Glue flat scallop shells face upwards to the bottom of the pot, first at the front, then at the back, and then the two sides, to ensure the pot stands straight.

4

Fill the pot with packing material and place a saucer on top of this. Stand a candle on the saucer.

5

Tie raffia around the pot where it joins the stand.

6

Decorate the stand with a few more cockles, if you like. Stand a few more curved scallop shells inside the original row to create a fuller, more petalled shape.

Shell Mirror

The subtle rose-pinks of ordinary scallop shells, picked up from the fishmonger, make for an easy, eye-catching mirror surround that's also environmentally friendly. Here, four large ones have been used at the corners with smaller ones filling in the sides.

MATERIALS

sandpaper
mirror in wooden frame
paint
paintbrush
4 large flat scallop shells
hot glue gun and glue sticks
10 small flat scallop shells
seagrass string
2 metal eyelets

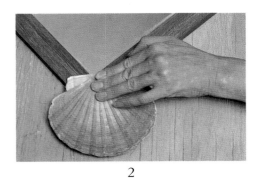

1

Sand down and paint the mirror frame with the colour of your choice.

2

Position the large scallop shells at the corners of the mirror, using the hot glue.

3

In the same way, glue three of the smaller scallop shells to each side of the mirror.

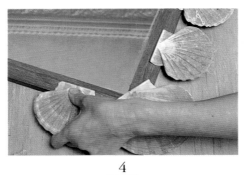

4

Attach two of the smaller scallop shells to the top of the mirror and two to the bottom.

5

Plait three lengths of seagrass string to make a hanger.

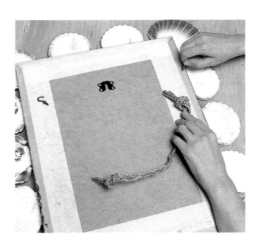

6

Screw metal eyelets into each side of the frame at the back, and tie the hanger on to these.

Chicken-wire Heart

*The garden shed provided the materials for this heart. Two shapes are simply cut
from chicken-wire and joined to give a more three-dimensional effect; then
they are decorated with string. The heart is lovely hung on the wall inside;
if it is decorated with a heavy-duty garden string it could also be hung outside.*

MATERIALS

*newspaper for template
scissors
chicken-wire
wire cutters or secateurs
paper string or any strong string*

1

Cut a heart template about 35 cm / 14 in long
from newspaper. Use this as a pattern to cut
two heart shapes from chicken-wire.

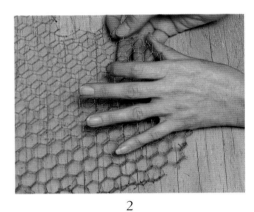

2

Place one chicken-wire heart on top of the
other, and bend in the edges sharply all
round to join the shapes.

3

Thread strong string all around the edges
to finish, leaving two long ends free at the
centre. Thread a separate piece of string at
the centre top, and tie the ends together to
make a hanging loop.

Raffia Heart

*This charming heart starts life, somewhat inauspiciously, as a coat hanger.
With the hook cut off, the hanger is simply bent to shape, ready to be wrapped
with raffia. A similar tiny heart, made from heavy-gauge reel wire, is hung in
the centre to finish it off.*

1

Bend the coat hanger into a heart shape
and cut off the hook.

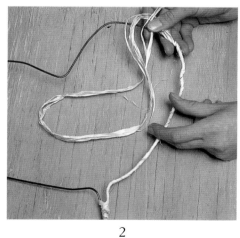

2

Starting at the base of the heart and leaving
a free length of raffia, wind raffia around the
heart to meet in the middle again. Tie the
two ends together.

3

Make a smaller heart from wire and bind it
with raffia. Use raffia to tie the smaller heart
so that it hangs inside the larger one.
Tie a hanging loop on to the larger heart.

Natural Stationery

Add your own personal style to a simple brown-paper stationery folder or notebook, by making closures from anything to hand. Here, an auger-shell and a bundle of cinnamon sticks make elegant toggles, with loops made from twine and raffia.

*plain buff stationery folder
or notebook
auger-shell or cinnamon stick
upholstery needle
raffia or twine
hot glue gun and glue sticks
2 small squares of brown paper*

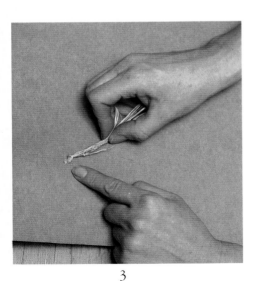

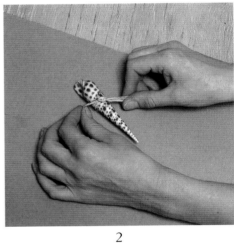

1

Work out the best position on the stationery folder or notebook for the shell or cinnamon stick toggle. Using an upholstery needle, pierce a hole in this position. Pass a loop of raffia through this to the front. Pass a short piece of raffia through this loop.

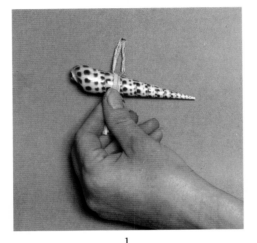

2

Tie the short piece of raffia around the shell or cinnamon stick. Secure it with a spot of glue.

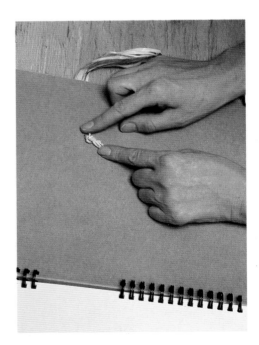

4

On the back cover, make a hole in a similar position to the one on the front cover. Thread a loop of raffia through this. Test the length by bringing it round to the front and experimenting with 'buttoning' and 'unbuttoning' the shell or stick, bearing in mind you will need extra slack to allow for knotting the loop in place. Make a knot in the raffia on the inside.

3

Open the folder or notebook. Tie a knot in the raffia close to the cover. Trim the ends.

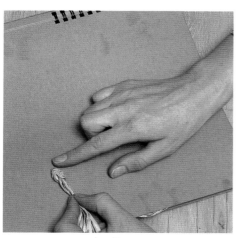

5

Close the folder or book and make another knot close to the cover on the outside so the loop is fixed firmly. Test the loop for size again, and if necessary, undo the knots and re-knot them in the right place.

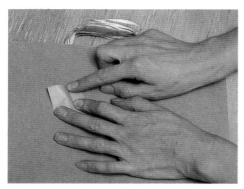

6

Cover the knots on the insides of the covers by gluing on the small squares of brown paper to avoid damage to the adjoining pages. This is also useful if you are using material for the loop that could stain the pages, such as coloured twine or a leather thong.

Filigree Leaf Wrap

Even the most basic brown parcel-paper can take on a very special look. Use a gilded skeletonized leaf and gold twine in combination with brown paper: chunky coir string would give a more robust look.

MATERIALS

picture framer's wax gilt
large skeletonized leaf
brown paper
sticky tape
gold twine
hot glue gun and glue sticks,
if necessary

1

Rub wax gilt into the skeletonized leaf.

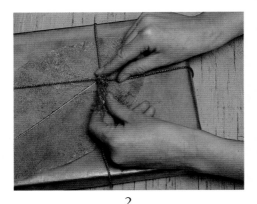

2

Wrap the parcel in the brown paper and rub gilt wax on to the corners. Tie the parcel with gold twine, bringing the two ends together and tying a knot. Fray the ends to create a tassle effect. Slip the leaf under the twine, securing it with glue at each end if necessary.

Fruit and Foliage Gift-wraps

Here, gilded brown parcel-paper provides a fitting background for a decoration of leaves and dried fruit slices.

MATERIALS

brown paper
sticky tape
picture framer's wax gilt
seagrass string
hot glue gun and glue sticks
dried fruit slices
preserved leaves

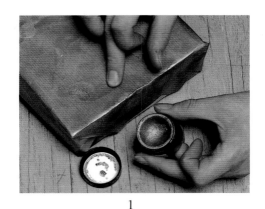

1

Wrap the parcel with brown paper and rub in gilt wax, paying special attention to the corners.

2

Tie the parcel with seagrass string, and then glue a different dried fruit or leaf to each quarter.

Tissue Rosette Gift-wrap

*Tissue papers make a fabulous foundation for any gift-wrapping; they come in
a glorious array of colours, and they softly take to any shape.*

MATERIALS

*tissue paper in 2 shades
co-ordinating twine*

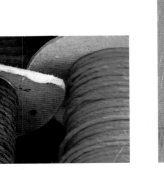

1

Place a cylindrical gift in the centre of two
squares of tissue, one laid on top of the other.
Gather the tissue up and tie it with twine.

2

Gently open out the rosette at the top.

Lavender Tissue Gift-wrap

*Bunches of lavender add a real country touch to tissue gift-wrap,
and become part of the gift.*

MATERIALS

*dried lavender
twine
tissue paper in 2 shades
sticky tape
glue*

1

Make two bunches of lavender and tie them
with twine to form a cross.

2

Wrap the parcel in the darker toned tissue
paper, and then wrap it with the paler tissue,
cut to form an envelope. Glue the lavender
to the front of the parcel.

Bath-time Bottle

Recycle a glass bottle containing home-made lotion and decorate it with corrugated card in gem-like colours for a real impact.

MATERIALS

*scissors
coloured corrugated card
flower-water bottle
hot glue gun and glue sticks
coloured raffia*

1

Cut the corrugated card to size, and then glue in position around the bottle. Tie with raffia.

2

Make a matching label from corrugated card, and tie it on using raffia.

Bath-time Treat Jar

Decorate a jar of lotion to complement the bottle, using brilliantly coloured fine corrugated card. Royal blue and emerald green make a rich combination that could be used for both men and women.

MATERIALS

*scissors
coloured corrugated card
baby-food jar
hot glue gun and glue sticks
twine*

1

Cut the corrugated card to size, and then glue in place around the jar. Tie the twine around the jar.

2

Cut a piece of corrugated card to fit the top of the lid and glue it in place. Glue twine to cover the side of the lid.

Wooden Candlesticks

This pair of matching wooden candlesticks have been made from old balusters that were removed from a stair rail. This is an easy way to make something from turned wood without having to operate a lathe yourself. Balusters can be bought singly from wood merchants or DIY stores.

The only special equipment needed is a vice and a flat-head drill bit, to make a hole in the top of the baluster large enough to hold a candle.

The candlesticks have been painted in bright earthy colours, giving a matching pair fit to grace any country table.

MATERIALS

*saw
2 wooden balusters (reclaimed or new)
2 square wood off-cuts
medium- and fine-grade sandpaper
wood glue
vice*

*electric drill fitted with a flat-head drill bit
acrylic paint in bright yellow, red and raw umber or burnt sienna
household and artist's brushes
clear matt acrylic varnish
soft clean cloth*

1

Cut out the most interesting section of the baluster and a square base; this one measures 7.5 × 7.5 cm / 3 × 3 in. Roughen the bottom of the baluster with sandpaper.

2

Very slightly, chamfer the base with fine-grade sandpaper. Glue the two sections together with wood glue.

3

Hold the candlestick securely in the vice and drill a hole for the candle 2 cm / ¾ in in diameter and 2 cm / ¾ in deep.

4

Paint with two or three coats of bright yellow acrylic paint.

5

Apply a coat of orange acrylic paint (add a touch of red to the yellow acrylic).

6

Tint the varnish to a muddy brown, by adding a squeeze of raw umber or burnt sienna. Brush this over the orange.

7

Use a crumpled cloth to lift some varnish and reveal the colour below.

CAUTION

When using wooden candlesticks do not leave burning candles unattended or allow the candle to burn right down, as the wood may catch fire.

Rosemary-flavoured Oil

This pungent oil is ideal drizzled over meat or vegetables before grilling.

INGREDIENTS

600 ml / 1 pint / 2 1/2 cups olive oil
5 fresh rosemary sprigs

Makes 600 ml / 1 pint / 2 1/2 cups

—1—

Heat the oil until warm but not too hot.

—2—

Add four rosemary sprigs and heat gently. Put the reserved rosemary sprig in a clean bottle. Strain the oil, pour in the bottle and seal tightly. Allow to cool and store in a cool, dark place. Use within a week.

Thyme-flavoured Vinegar

This vinegar is delicious sprinkled over salmon intended for poaching.

INGREDIENTS

600 ml / 1 pint / 2 1/2 cups
white-wine vinegar
5 fresh thyme sprigs
3 garlic cloves, peeled

Makes 600 ml / 1 pint / 2 1/2 cups

—1—

Warm the vinegar.

—2—

Add four thyme sprigs and the garlic and heat gently. Put the reserved thyme sprig in a clean bottle, strain the vinegar, and add to the bottle. Seal tightly, allow to cool and store in a cool, dark place. The vinegar may be kept unopened for up to 3 months.

Index